THE SCHOOL GARDEN

Reason with Shapes and Their Attributes

Sebastian Avery

NEW YORK

Published in 2015 by The Rosen Publishing Group, Inc.
29 East 21st Street, New York, NY 10010

Book Design: Jonathan J. D'Rozario

Photo Credits: Cover Ivonne Wierink/Shutterstock.com; pp. 3,4,6–24 (Background) J.D.S/Shutterstock.com;
p. 5 DeepGreen/Shutterstock.com; p. 7 Catalin Petolea/Shutterstock.com; p. 9 aboikis/Shutterstock.com;
p. 11 Henk Jacobs/Shutterstock.com; p. 13 Alison Hancock/Shutterstock.com; p.15 FotograFFF/Shutterstock.com;
p. 17 Ta Khum/Shutterstock.com; p. 19 Gregory Johnston/Shutterstock.com; p. 21 joloei/Shutterstock.com;
p. 22 paulaphoto/ Shutterstock.com.

Library of Congress Cataloging-in-Publication Data

Avery, Sebastian, author.
The school garden : reason with shapes and their attributes / Sebastian Avery.
    pages cm. — (Math masters. Geometry)
Includes index.
ISBN 978-1-4777-4875-6 (pbk.)
ISBN 978-1-4777-4874-9 (6-pack)
ISBN 978-1-4777-6470-1 (library binding)
1. Geometry—Juvenile literature. 2. Shapes—Juvenile literature. 3. School gardens—Juvenile literature. I. Title.
QA445.5.A93 2015
516—dc23
                        2014009619

Manufactured in the United States of America

CPSIA Compliance Information: Batch #WS15RC: For further information contact Rosen Publishing, New York, New York at 1-800-237-9932.

CONTENTS

A CLASS PROJECT

It's the beginning of a new school year, and my teacher wants to start a big **project** for our class. We decide to **organize** a school garden! This will help us make new friends in class and meet people from other classes, too.

Our principal says we can use a **plot** of land behind the school for our garden. We can **partition** this land into smaller parts with equal areas. Then, each class can use one of those equal sections for their garden. They can grow whatever they'd like!

Some students want to grow vegetables and fruit, and other students want to grow flowers. I want to grow zucchini because it's my favorite food!

5

We have to get the garden ready before we can plant anything. We have to make sure the garden is in a spot with lots of sun and good soil.

We partition the garden into equal sections. Equal parts of a whole can be written as fractions. We know the parts are equal because they're the same size, which means they have the same area. This whole garden has an area of 16 square units. A unit square is a square whose sides have a length of 1 unit. It's used to measure area.

We cut the whole garden into 4 smaller, equal sections. Each section has an area of 4 square units. That means each of the 4 sections is the same size as the other sections. Because these 4 smaller parts have the same area, each one makes up $\frac{1}{4}$ of the whole square.

$\dfrac{1}{4}$

7

FRESH VEGETABLES

Each class takes their own plot of land. Miss Smith's class wants to plant vegetables so they can **harvest** and eat them. They might have enough to share with others. They decide to plant carrots and turnips.

Miss Smith's class has a plot that's shaped like a rectangle. First, they plan their garden on paper with a **grid**. The rectangle's area is 12 square units, and they partition it into 3 equal sections. The sections are equal because each has an area of 4 square units. Each section is $\frac{1}{3}$ of the whole plot.

There are 2 same-size sections for carrots and 1 section for turnips. That means turnips take up $\frac{1}{3}$ of the whole plot. The carrots take up $\frac{2}{3}$ of the plot.

carrots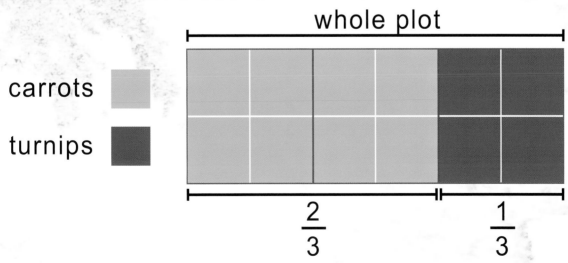

turnips

whole plot

$\dfrac{2}{3}$ $\dfrac{1}{3}$

9

Mr. Perry wants to use gardening to teach his students about photosynthesis (foh-toh-SIHN-thuh-suhs), which is how plants make their food. Beans grow quickly, so they're good examples to use.

Mr. Perry's class has a plot that's a rectangle, and they decide to grow 6 different kinds of beans. First, they partition the plot into 6 equal sections. One section is for lima beans. The area of the lima bean section is $\frac{1}{6}$ of the area of the whole plot. They can make 6 equal sections in 2 different ways.

If you make 2 columns and 3 rows, there are 6 equal sections. If you make 3 columns and 2 rows, there are 6 equal sections, too. Each section has an area that's $\frac{1}{6}$ of the area of the whole rectangle.

$$\frac{1}{6}$$

$$\frac{1}{6}$$

 lima bean = $\frac{1}{6}$

11

Miss Lawley's students are going to grow an herb (UHRB) garden. Herbs are plants that can be used for flavoring food, and some are even used for medicine. Some herbs are used fresh, and others are dried. They'll grow basil, parsley, and thyme.

Miss Lawley's class partitions their rectangular plot into 8 equal sections. They can partition it with 2 columns and 4 rows, or with 2 rows and 4 columns. Either way, they get 8 equal parts of the whole rectangle. What fraction of the plot is for basil?

There are 3 sections for basil, and each section equals $\frac{1}{8}$. That means the area of the basil section is $\frac{3}{8}$ of the area of the whole plot.

$\frac{1}{8}$

$\frac{1}{8}$

$\frac{1}{8}$

$\frac{1}{8}$ $\frac{1}{8}$ $\frac{1}{8}$

■ basil = $\frac{3}{8}$

13

BEAUTIFUL FLOWERS

Some classes want to grow flowers. Flowers **attract** different kinds of bugs, such as butterflies, ladybugs, and honeybees.

The students in Mrs. McKee's class decide to make their plot a circle. You can't partition a circle with columns and rows because not all the sections would be the same. You need to partition circles from the center, like when you cut a pie. Each part must be the same size. The students partition the circle into 3 equal parts. They'll grow a different-colored flower in each part.

The circle has 1 part for yellow pansies, 1 part for pink pansies, and 1 part for blue pansies. Each color flower takes up $\frac{1}{3}$ of the area of the whole plot.

blue pansies = $\frac{1}{3}$

pink pansies = $\frac{1}{3}$

yellow pansies = $\frac{1}{3}$

Some people make gardens with special flowers that attract butterflies. These are called butterfly gardens. The flowers in butterfly gardens are colorful and have nectar that butterflies like to eat. Nectar is the sweet juice inside a flower.

Mr. Sutton's class is going to make their plot a circle, too. They'll partition it into 10 equal sections and sprinkle seeds over the soil. They sprinkle cosmos seeds over 4 sections, marigold seeds over 2 sections, and daisy seeds over 4 sections.

How much of the circle plot will have cosmos? You can add $\frac{1}{10}$ four times to get an answer of $\frac{4}{10}$. Cosmos cover $\frac{4}{10}$ of the total area of the butterfly garden. Notice that $\frac{4}{10}$ is the same as $\frac{2}{5}$.

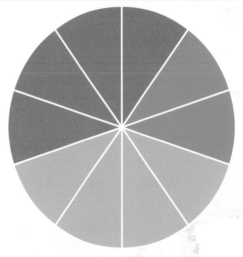

cosmos = $\frac{4}{10}$

marigolds = $\frac{2}{10}$

daisies = $\frac{4}{10}$

OUR GARDEN

Most classes used their plots to make gardens shaped like rectangles and circles. But my teacher wants us to learn about partitioning other shapes. My class has 2 plots. We're using 1 plot to make a garden that's shaped like an equilateral triangle.

A triangle is a shape with 3 sides. An equilateral triangle can be split into 4 smaller equilateral triangles that are all the same size. We make equal parts for onions, garlic, kale, and spinach. Onions and garlic are bulb vegetables. Kale and spinach are leaf vegetables.

What fraction of our triangle plot has leaf vegetables on it? There are 2 sections out of 4 that have leaf vegetables. That means leaf vegetables take up $\frac{2}{4}$ of the area of the plot. Notice that $\frac{2}{4}$ is the same as $\frac{1}{2}$.

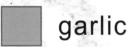 garlic

 spinach

kale

onions

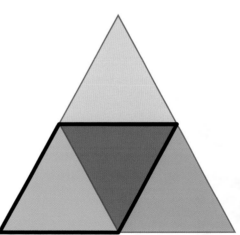

19

Our other plot is going to be for flowers. My teacher wants it to be shaped like a hexagon. A hexagon is a shape that has 6 sides. We're going to partition it into 6 equilateral triangles. Each triangle will equal $\frac{1}{6}$ of the total area of the hexagon.

We decide to plant roses. We have to buy them at the store. We use 2 sections for pink roses, 2 for yellow roses, and 2 for orange roses. What fraction of the plot has yellow roses?

There are 2 equal triangles for yellow roses. So, I know that yellow roses take up $\frac{2}{6}$ of the area of the hexagon plot. That's the same as $\frac{1}{3}$ of the plot.

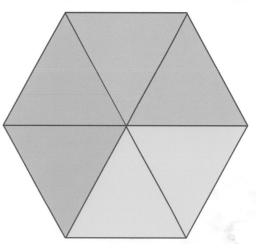

yellow roses

pink roses

orange roses

PLAN YOUR OWN!

Making a school garden was a lot of work, but it was worth it! Many students and teachers came together to make the garden a success. The flowers filled the garden with color and attracted butterflies. We were even able to harvest some of the vegetables to use for snacks!

It's important to plan what you want your garden to look like before you start. What shape do you want it to be? You can partition your shape into smaller sections to include different vegetables and flowers.

GLOSSARY

attract (uh-TRAKT) To cause to come near.

grid (GRIHD) A set of lines that cross each other to make

squares of equal size.

harvest (HAHR-vuhst) To gather crops.

organize (OHR-guh-nyz) To bring together for a task or activity.

partition (pahr-TIH-shun) To break something into parts.

plot (PLAHT) An area of land.

project (PRAH-jehkt) A task.

INDEX

Due to the changing nature of Internet links, The Rosen Publishing Group, Inc., has developed an online list of websites related to the subject of this book. This site is updated regularly. Please use this link to access the list: www.powerkidslinks.com/mm/geo/tsg